Crinkleroot's
NATURE GUIDES:

FOR MY SISTER, DONNA

SIMON & SCHUSTER BOOKS FOR YOUNG READERS
An imprint of Simon & Schuster Children's Publishing Division
1230 Avenue of the Americas, New York, New York 10020

Text and illustrations copyright © 1997 by Jim Arnosky
SIMON & SCHUSTER BOOKS FOR YOUNG READERS
is a trademark of Simon & Schuster.
The text for this book is set in Bookman Medium.
The illustrations are rendered in watercolor.
Printed and bound in the United States of America
First Edition
1 3 5 7 9 10 8 6 4 2

Library of Congress Cataloging-in-Publication Data
Arnosky, Jim.
Crinkleroot's guide to knowing animal habitats
by Jim Arnosky.—1st ed.
p.   cm.
Summary : Introduces different wildlife habitats,
including wetlands, woodlands, cornfields, and grasslands.
ISBN 978-1-4814-2599-5
1. Habitat (Ecology)—Juvenile literature. [1. Habitat (Ecology)]
I. Title.
QH541.14.A75   1997   591.5—dc20   96-19226

Crinkleroot's
GUIDE TO KNOWING
ANIMAL HABITATS
BY JIM ARNOSKY

Simon & Schuster Books for Young Readers

Hello! My name is Crinkleroot. I'm an explorer and a wildlife finder. I've found so many wild creatures sharing this sweet earth, I lost count somewhere around a billion!

MUSQUASH

I see so many wild critters because I know where they all live. The natural places where wild animals live are called habitats.

I'm going to visit lots of different wildlife habitats. You can come too!

The first place I want to show you
is a watery place, or wetland.

CROSS SECTION OF A WETLAND:

MUD

WATER TABLE (WATER LEVEL IN SOIL)

SAND, PEBBLES, AND STONES.

A wetland is any place where water is near, at, or just above the surface of the ground. You may have a tiny wetland in your own backyard where the soil is always moist and the grass grows more lush.

NOTE: SOME TYPES OF WETLANDS ARE NOT FIRM ENOUGH TO WALK ON. THE BEST WAY TO OBSERVE MOST WETLANDS IS IN THE COMPANY OF AN ADULT AND FROM THE SAFETY OF HIGHER GROUND OR A STURDY BOARDWALK.

The three most common wetlands are marshes, swamps, and bogs. A marsh is full of tall grasses, cattails, and reeds. Here water is above ground in many spots.

CANADA GEESE

GREAT BLUE HERON

MERGANSERS

PAINTED TURTLE

RED-WINGED BLACKBIRD

MALLARDS

BULLFROG

MUSKRAT

ANHINGA

EGRET

OTTER

ALLIGATOR

A swamp is a place where many woody plants grow and water covers nearly all the land.

MUD TURTLE

LITTLE BLUE HERON

WATER MOCCASIN

A bog is a place where the land actually floats on water.

MOOSE

The shallow water of any wetland is a world of plants, rocks, sand, and sunken trees.

SUNFISH

NEWT

DAMSELFLY
LARVA

FRESHWATER
MUSSEL

WATER
BOATMAN

CRAYFISH

DRAGONFLY
LARVA

MINNOWS

MADTOM

It is a rich weedy habitat for underwater wildlife.

PICKEREL

SNAPPING
TURTLE

In a woodland, tree trunks, stems, and branches criss-cross and overlap. It takes sharp eyes to pick out even the noisiest creatures, like hammering woodpeckers or chirping red squirrels. But make no mistake! Any woodland is habitat for a variety of wildlife. For every animal you hear or see, there are many more hiding.

WHITE-BREASTED NUTHATCH

RED
SQUIRREL

GREAT
HORNED
OWL

In the woods, animals may be living high in the treetops, in middle branches or trunks, or on the woodland floor.

See if you can find the wildlife living
in this little patch of woods. (I'll give
you a hint: there are twenty-four in all.
Twenty-seven if you count walking
stick, Sassafrass, and me.)

Climb aboard my old jalopy! There are some interesting places I want to show you that are miles apart. Along the way, we're sure to spot some wildlife near the road.

CROWS

RING-NECKED PHEASANT

DEER

WOODCHUCK

Rabbits, deer, woodchucks, and other normally shy animals come out to the roadsides to feed on lush green plants growing in the open sunlight.

Roadsides are also hunting grounds for hungry crows, hawks, and kestrels.

RED-TAILED HAWK

KESTREL

35 MPH

NATURE

RABBIT

Our first stop is a farmer's cornfield. Cornfields provide an ever-changing habitat for wildlife. In the spring gulls, swallows, and bluebirds feed on beetles, grubs, and earthworms unearthed by the farmer's plow.

By midsummer, when the corn stalks have grown high enough to provide cover, small animals move in to nest and raise their young.

At ripening time the cornfield becomes a supermarket for raiding raccoons.

By late fall, after the field of corn has been freshly cut and harvested, the scattered kernels are a feast for migrating geese.

MOST SMALL GRASSLAND ANIMALS ARE BIRDS OR BURROWERS—OR BOTH!

From small hillside meadows to vast rolling plains, grasslands are wide open spaces where wildlife can thrive.

GOLDFINCH

MONARCH BUTTERFLY

TICK

WHEN WALKING IN GRASSLAND, STOP TO CHECK YOUR CLOTHES FOR TICKS. TICKS ARE NUMEROUS IN TALL GRASS.

YOU'LL FIND MORE KINDS OF INSECTS AND SPIDERS IN GRASSLANDS THAN IN ANY OTHER HABITAT.

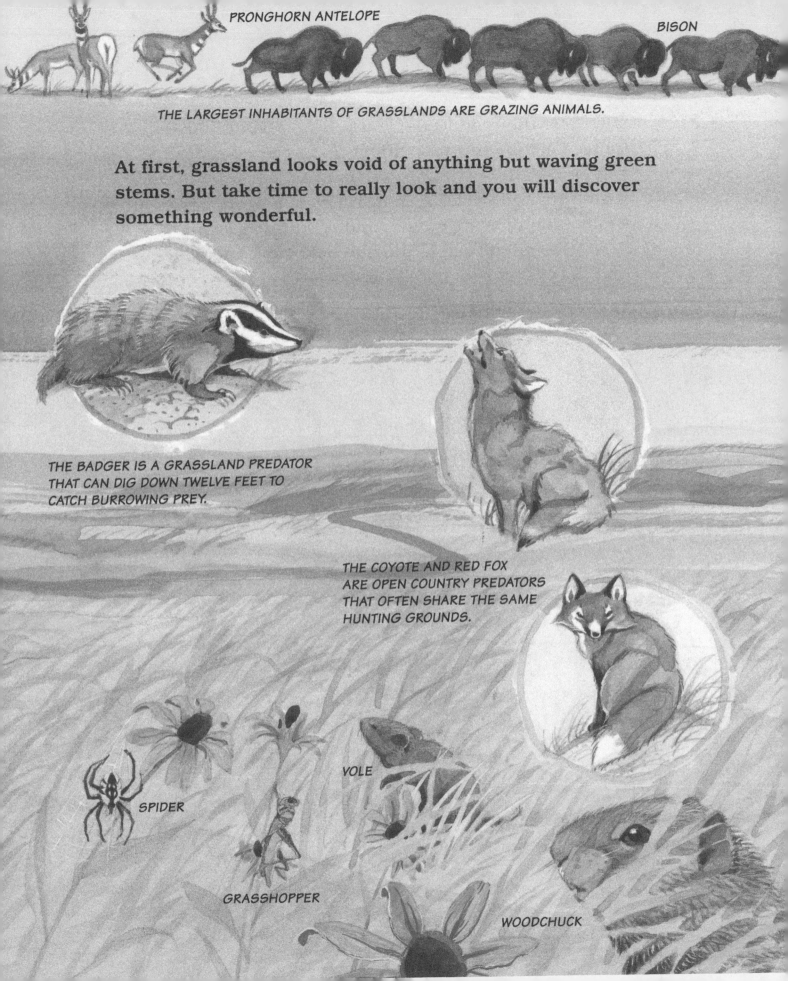

PRONGHORN ANTELOPE

BISON

THE LARGEST INHABITANTS OF GRASSLANDS ARE GRAZING ANIMALS.

At first, grassland looks void of anything but waving green stems. But take time to really look and you will discover something wonderful.

THE BADGER IS A GRASSLAND PREDATOR THAT CAN DIG DOWN TWELVE FEET TO CATCH BURROWING PREY.

THE COYOTE AND RED FOX ARE OPEN COUNTRY PREDATORS THAT OFTEN SHARE THE SAME HUNTING GROUNDS.

SPIDER

VOLE

GRASSHOPPER

WOODCHUCK

Wherever the road leads, you will find wildlife living there. Even the hottest, driest places can be home to animals. In the drylands, wildlife find cover behind sage brush and cactus, beneath rock ledges, or for some, simply by digging in and covering up with sand. Succulent plants provide both food and water. And for predators, there is prey.

HERE IS A SAMPLING OF THE MANY WILDLIFE SPECIES THAT INHABIT DRYLANDS FROM SAGE BRUSH COUNTRY TO DESERT SANDS.

MULE DEER

ARMADILLO

KANGAROO RAT

JACKRABBIT

DIAMONDBACK RATTLESNAKE

ROADRUNNER

COLLARED LIZARD

BROAD-BILLED HUMMINGBIRD

HORNED LIZARD

ELF OWL

RAVEN

MUSKRATS

NATURE

PIKA

Learn to recognize the different wildlife habitats, from low-lands to mountains, wetlands to drylands. Don't be fooled by how small a place may be. Some wild critters get by in surprisingly little space—a bit of brush, a swampy puddle, a pile of rocks, a tiny woodlot, or a lone cactus.

Well now! I told you we'd cover a lot of territory and we did! I counted over eighty different wildlife species on our trip. How many did you count? I hope you enjoyed the journey. I did. So did Sassafrass. She always likes riding in the old jalopy. We'll see you soon. Until then, remember, wherever you go, you share the world with wildlife.

BIGHORN
SHEEP